BOONAGE SE

ADITYA AMAN JHA

Contents

Preface

"BOONAGE" is written by a teenager like you all. He has faced all these major problems in his teen and even facing so many others till now. He wanted to correlate with all the teenagers who are facing problems mentioned in the book. I hope he will be able to correlate with all of you and help you to solve the problems. Let's jorney together from TEENAGE to BOONAGE.

THANKYOU

Acknowledgements

SPECIAL THANKS TO SHRINIDHI JHA (EDITOR)

CHAPTER ONE

Who Am I ?

So after reading 'Before You Read', all of you must have come to know that I am also a teenager like all of you. And mainly I am not writing this book for fun or for time pass, rather I am writing this book for all those teenagers who consider themselves as ordinary like me. And as I think of myself, he also thinks of himself the same way.

If to be straight, I am not writing a book to give advice or suggestions like other people say, but I am trying my best to do what I have experienced or whatever my teenage has lived with you. And I can claim that when you reach the last page of this book, you will learn to manage yourself to a great extent and maybe we will become close friends on this journey and I will also learn a lot from you. I will make you feel that this is not only the Author's Book, this is the Book of a teenager who can be anyone.

So the rest of the things will continue to happen in the journey of this ten confluence, but first of all it is very important for us to know that why did we name this book "BOONAGE"? And second, the name of the first chapter of the book is "WHO I AM?" Why is it?

So first of all, I named this book "BOONAGE" because the era in which we are living is not just a normal time period. It is the time which gives you the long lasting memories, nostalgic feelings, your freedom, your progress and so many other things. We can't take this age so simple. This is a major part of our life. We must feel glad that we got it in our life.

Be Pleased.....

TEENAGE is BOONAGE. The era which proves to be BOON for us. But, there are some terms and conditions applied on this as well. If you live your teenage in some limitations then it proves to be boon but if you start enjoying your freedom more than the need, it may start punishing you. This book "BOONAGE" is completely based on the frame of our life and building up our attitude and personality. So that, you can achieve the thing which you want and you deserve as well. It will even boost your confidence to make your future better.

So, Come On, let us feel the book...!

Now, the another major question.
Why our first chapter is: "WHO AM I?"

Before moving further and discussing about the frames and building blocks our of teenage, we must know about ourselves. We must ask this question to ourselves "Who Am I ?"

This is not a funny question for which you will answer that I am ...., My father's name is ...., My mother's name is..... and so on.

This question is really serious and I am pretty sure, you will find solutions of your so many problems from this single question.

Just ask this question to yourself:
• Who Am I?
• What I can do?
• Why God has send me to the earth?
• what are my ambitions?

These questions will give answer to thousands of the questions which get emerged in your mind.

"मैं कौन हूँ?"

मैं...

मैं वो हूँ

जो दिखिता तो हूँ

पर हर बार नजरअंदाज किया जाता हूँ

मैं एक किशोर,

आज का शहजादा,

और आने वाले कल का राजा हूँ।

मैं उस ताले की चाभी हूँ

जो बंद तकदीरे खोलता हौ

मैं उस समय का फेरा हूँ

जो हर बार अपना राह बदलता हौ।

मैं उस भगवान् का वास्ता हूँ

जो हर घर में बसता हैं

और उसे अक्सर माता–पिता के नाम से पुकारा जाता हौ।

मैं वो हूँ..

जो हर छोटी–छोटी बातों पर गुस्सा हो जाता हूँ

लेकिन थोडी दरे बाद खुद सब समझ जाता हूँ

पर अक्सर अफसोस के छाए में बंधा रह जाता हूँ।

मैं वो हूँ..

जो एक देश का भविष्य बना सकता हौ

मैं वो भी हूँ..
जो पूरे कायनात को डूबा सकता हूँ।

हैं अनंत मेरी शक्तियाँ,
तुम मुझे रोक नहीं सकते।

हैं दम तो मुझे रोक लो
मेरा कदम चट्टानों को चीर कर भी अपना रास्ता बना लेता हूँ।

मैं एक किशोर,
आज का शहजादा,
और आने वाले कल का राजा हूँ।

– आदित्य अमन झा
"WHO AM I?"
I...
I am that
what I see,
But every time I get ignored.

I'm a teenager
Today's prince
And I am the king of tomorrow.

I am the key to that lock,
One who opens closed fortunes.

i'm in that time
The one who changes his path every time.

I belong to that god

who lives in every house
And he is often called by the name of the parent.

I am that...
I get angry over every little thing.

But after a while I understand everything myself
But often I am tied in the shadow of pity.

I am that...
Who can make the future of a country.

I am that too...
Which can drown the whole universe.

my powers are infinite,
you can not stop me.

If you dare, stop me
My step makes its way even by tearing rocks.

I'm a teenager
Today's prince
And I am the king of tomorrow.

- Aditya Aman Jha

This poetry has a great depth in itself. When you read it with complete focus, you will find that this poem is a mirror to the teenagers life who have a lot of expectations from themselves. Somewhere, this poem explains the thoughts of teenagers and their strength as well.

Who they are and what they can do!

So this is it for this chapter. We will meet very soon in the next chapter with one of the most lesson for all of us.

CHAPTER TWO

Belief System

Now here a question arises, why we have chosen "BELIEF SYSTEM" as our first step towards turning teen into boon?

If we once look back at our teenager, then the biggest drawback we will see in ourselves is not having any believe in ourselves. We always think that I am wrong, I am doing wrong, I can't achieve anything, I am loser, the person in front of me or my classmates are correct, I am nothing in front of them and bla bla bla..... . This thing defeats us even before we fight.

We have often heard a story about the elephant and the king of the jungle, the lion from our childhood.Elephants are way heavier than lions but when there is a fight between them, lion always wins! We also know the reason why this happens, but we never try to apply this rule in our life. We always take this as light as a piece of paper which can easily be blown by a gust of wind. Lions have believe on themselves that they can easily defeat the elephants while, the elephants always think like us that they can't do anything and easily get defeated by the lions. But, we know what the truth is, who can win or who can lose!

So, this chapter will teach us how we can strengthen our inner belief system. LET'S GO!!!

Do you guys actually know, what is the meaning of "BELIEF SYSTEM"? It's not that which we expect or we understand, it's totally different. We think "BELIEF SYSTEM" means believe on yourself. But no, "BELIEF SYSTEM" means the believe on your soul. Your soul never disappoints you, it can never take you down or discourage you. If you ask a question from your inner soul, " Can I do this?" The answer will definitely be "yes".

Now here again a question arises, what is "soul"?
It's answer is simple but little twisty. All the yogasanas and meditations, for whose peace do you do all these? Some people will say for peace of heart, some will say for peace of mind but no, you all do this for the peace of your soul, your inner soul, that inspires you to do good deeds and you do too.

So the main lesson from this para is, always listen to your soul, it will never discourage you. If you think you are doing something wrong, just sit in a corner with nothing ,i.e., phone, book or anything else and close your eyes and ask just a single question from your soul, "am I doing anything wrong?" And hope so you will get the answer.

The second most important thing you all must need to follow is "The Best Never Competes." Don't try to compare yourself with anyone else. Always feel yourself unique, you are the one who can change everything. Just feel the power of a teenager, power of a growing tree. Just make a simple principle in your life that, " I am never gonna compete myself with anyone but yeah, I will follow the good deeds and ideals.

Once in an interview, A great Indian buisnessman had said that, " I make my decision correct after taking it." So, it's my words to all of you guys, trust on your decision and on your deeds. What happen if we will lose, We will at least get a gift to learn something and very soon we will comeback with great power. Let the fear of losing be blown and be yourself.

• Always trust yourself rather than the other person.
• If you can dream, you can achieve.

CHAPTER THREE

Influence

Let us start this chapter again with a question, why we have chosen "INFLUENCE" as our second step towards turning teen into boon?

So far we have seen that when we are in our teenage, we have very less confidence and believe on ourselves, we always rely on others rather to rely on our own. In this cycle, we start getting influenced by others to make ourselves better. We start trying to copy our fellow whom we think are better from us. Urge to be popular in our surrounding compel us to copy them and we do this too. We have to understand this that there is a huge difference between copying and following. Also, why don't we have to be influenced towards other?

This chapter takes you one step ahead towards your journey to change and you will enjoy this too. Let's go!!!

As we enter our teen years, we get a new haunt of copying artists from the flim industry and some other people as well. We are like, aww! He is very handsome or aww! She is very beautiful and from here to be on that place, we gradually start copying them, we get influenced towards them. I am not saying that copying someone is totally wrong, but yeah! It's also not totally correct.We want to imitate a person's present, we never want to imitate his past hardwork and restless consistency, even we don't try to do this.Present of a successful person is not successful rather his restless past, hardworking past and consistent focused past is successful.

We easily get influenced to a person and start imitating them. We don't think that we are unique and we have some special abilities. We can do a lot better then any other person. We should obey the principles of somebody (ideal) in life but, simply getting influenced is not beneficial. It is so much harsh that it can ruin our life upto large extent.

Nowadays we the generation of teenagers are more interested in doing such things which take very less time and can be done quickly.We do not want to spend too much time on any of our work. We want our work to be finished as soon as possible and then we start doing some other work.It has a very bad effect on our life, as well as the quality of the work we do is not very good.If you do not believe in this thing, then let's understand it with a real life example........

We see our favorite celebrities making videos on a short video making app. Seeing this thing, we get influenced and we also start making short videos on that app.For a time, if we are not influenced by any celebrity, then we get influenced by the friends around us who are making videos.So far it is fine that we are making short videos. Main problem arrives when we become habitual of this thing and leave our rest works for this. The point to note here is that making videos on that app is a source of income for our favorite celebrities, but for us, it's just a source of fun.Here some people will have the argument that many people are earning money through this, what about them! So listen, the number of people making money through it is very-very less than the number of people who are spending their time thinking that one day they will make money through it. Now, if you observe peacefully then, you will find that the main cause of destruction here in this case is none other than "INFLUENCE".

I (your inner soul) am saying again that anything is good for you and your future to a limited extent, but as the effect of that thing increases, you and your future are in danger and I am also affected by it.

OTHERS CAN INFLUENCE YOU,
BUT THEY CAN'T INSPIRE YOU.

CHAPTER FOUR

Addiction

Keeping our customs ahead, we start this chapter again with a question. Here a question arises, why we have chosen "ADDICTION" as our third step towards turning teen into boon?

So far we have seen how in our teens we get influenced by others and start copying them. After Influence, the next step is Addiction, in which we become Habitual by following the Habit of the front. Our attention gets diverted from the rest of our work and we always want to do only that one thing. Because of this, many times we are also scolded by our parents and teachers, because most of the things we get addicted to in teenage are bad things. Now, here you will ask from me that how can I say this. So look, as a teenager, we often want to do the work which is easy and fun to do. Both these qualities are very well present in bad habits. On scolding by teachers and parents, we also ignore their point because we are living in such an age (teenage) where we get everyone's point wrong except one person's point......

All of this is not our fault. It's an age and we can't skip it. But, I make you assure that after reading this book

[BOONAGE], you will get rid of all your problems and live an ideal teenage life.

Now, let us make our concern towards the problem that how we can prevent addiction to things or we have become addicted to something, so how do we come out of it, even good things as well because everything is good upto a limit.

If you want that you should not be addicted to anything, then the most important emotional thing that should be inside you is "control over yourself". Let your inner soul control your body. Your inner soul will never make you addict to anything. If you listen to your inner soul, it will neither allow you to become addicted to any activity nor will it ever allow you to become addicted to any person. In the age in which we are living, an addiction which affects us in a very dirty way is "addiction to person". Many of you may not be able to understand what it means but must be suffering with this problem. Due to change in our mental state and thinking, we get addicted to people in teenage. Sometimes, it can be just one person. We wish that the person should always talk to only me, should not talk to anyone other than me.

"One and Only me.....!"

This is called "Addiction to Person". In this case, we feel very bad if it is not what we want and children like us, start crying and lose our expectations from life. Remember carefully, at this time, many times a voice comes from inside you that do not do this, do not do this, it is of no use but you let go this voice. For me, this voice is from my inner soul which can never allow me to do anything wrong. If you have control over yourself and you listen to your inner god- inner person- inner mate, then nothing can be your addiction. This will be your first step towards becoming "mature you".

Many of you must have a question that how do we know that the voice which is coming from inside us is right and wants our well being?

"Trust me,a lumberjack never attack on his own foot with axe for fun!"

Most of the time you will find that your inner person is against you and your wants. Thus, it wants to take you on a right path. Also, when you will do something good, your inner person will appreciate you for that. Thus, you are already on a right path.

It is a matter of avoiding addiction, but what should we do when we are already addicted to something?

People will often tell you this way to quit addiction that instead of quitting slowly, give up all the addiction at once. But it's not so easy to do. It requires a lot of will power and control over our own. There are various stages when you come across this procedure. At first you will not feel that this will happen to me, but then your will power will wake up and tell you that no, you can do this. After this you will start leaving your addiction but again after one or two days, you will get tired of it and want to resume your addiction. If you stop yourself at this point, then after this you will easily get rid of your addiction because this is the hardest stage. From here, your are king who can get rid of his addictions with a smile on his face.

You get birth and start living,
But it requires lot more
HARDWORK
to build an empire with your
PERSONALITY

CHAPTER FIVE

Chagrin

Continuing the tradition, let's start our chapter again with a question. This chapter is all about your furious emotions mainly "Aggressiveness and Impatience".

Now here a question arises, why we have chosen "CHAGRIN" as our fourth step towards turning teen into boon?

Before knowing the answer of this question, let us first understand what is the meaning of "CHAGRIN"?

CHAGRIN is all about frustrated emotions which can't be simply defined as aggressiveness and impatience. It is not an useless emotion or expression. In some cases CHAGRIN may cause you to learn about a particular thing or a particular person in depth.

Suppose you are very annoyed with one person(A) but there is a person(B) in front of you who tells you some such things about that person(A) which makes you feel guilty on your thinking about that person(A). In this situation, you get to know a person in depth. But,if we look at its negative side, it causes a great impact on your mental and physical health as well. One of the major problems which we face in our teenage is: "Getting irritated on small talks". When our parents scold us on this matter, we misunderstand them and all these things increase our frustration a lot. This whole procedure happens with me more than 100 times in a day. So, It is an important issue on which we should discuss. So, let's do it...

See, when you get very much frustrated, you don't want to listen to anyone, whoever it is, your friends, your parents. At this time, it would be best for you to sit in a quiet place and think about something other than the one thing you are frustrated with. Mainly try to do those works which makes you happy and you like to do the most. Even when you have had a scolding and you are getting angry, you should calm down and move away from there instead of replying from the front. You should start thinking on a different matter. This will help you to make your patience level efficient and will also play an important role in making you always happy. After an hour or two, when you calm down, then think back on the matter that caused you to become furious. I am sure you will start laughing on yourself that what you were doing. That was all useless.

Now, at this moment a question often comes into our mind that why I got furious at that moment. So, the reason is simply science.

How??

Due to the high secretion of adrenaline in our teens, we tend to get furious quickly and show our expressions on useless things. We can't do anything with this but we can control its side affects with our mindset and determination.

Be calm and composed in these matters.....

Let it understand that we can conquer over any type of

situation with our cool mind. If you want to see the examples around the world, look at it..

One of world most famous Indian cricketer, "M.S. DHONI" is well- known for his cool mind. He is generally called "CAPTAIN COOL". Because of his cool and focused mind, he is able to make good strategies during the game and because of these strategies, he had won so many trophies and games in his captaincy Career. He is not only one example in the world. There are also so many persons around the world who have achieved success with his calm steps.

There are many such people in the life of all of us who want to take advantage of our anger and get their work done. We need to be aware of these people. These people want their entertainment so they use us and we also do their entertainment. THAT'S IT...

But I don't want it to be just THAT'S IT for us. So next time be aware of these people and be happy.

I hope after this you will not get furious when your friend come and hit on your back and run away.

BE CALM

OTHERWISE ONE WILL MAKE YOU

FOOL ANY DAY.

CHAPTER SIX

Company

Do you know what is company? Why we need a company? Why it matters? How it affects us? Is it good or bad, in other words is it boon or ban? Is it really important?

I know you all are thinking why I have asked all these questions from you. Actually, In this lesson we are going to learn about the 3I's of "COMPANY" in our life. Now, what are the 3I's of "COMPANY"?

These are:

• IMPORTANCE

• IMPACT

• INVOLVEMENT

I have asked the questions mentioned above from you so that while reading the chapter, you all can relate with me. This is because "COMPANY" is the most important thing in a person's life. Not only in our teenage, but "COMPANY" is the most important necessity in our whole life. In our childhood, we had friends with whom we play games. In our teenage, we have classmates and friends near our homes with whom we study or do fun. In our college time, we will have batchmates with whom we will make assignments and work on various projects and this will continue for our lifetime. Here, friends in our childhood, classmates, batchmates, etc. all are the examples of

"COMPANY". So, before making friends, we need to know which type of company we need to follow and how the company of good or bad friends affects us.

So far, it is clear that why we have selected"COMPANY" as our one of the step towards turning teen into boon but till now it is not clear that why we have selected"COMPANY" as our fifth step towards turning teen into boon. So, let's have a look at it.

So far we have learnt about Addiction (4th chapter) and Chagrin(5th chapter) which influences the teenage life but there is an important role of one thing behind these two life lessons (Addiction and Chagrin). That is "COMPANY". We get addicted to anything by watching someone in our friends group, which is a kind of COMPANY. For example: In this age, we all have a friends group in which there must be a child who often show seriousness towards his studies and career. By watching his seriousness, gradually we also become serious towards our studies.

On the other hand, if there is a guy in our friends circle who smokes, somehow we get attracted towards him more quickly than first case and in some cases, we also start doing so. If you will observe the friends circle around you carefully, you will also find such examples.

Here you can easily see that how friends group around us plays an important role in our growth and at the same time in our destruction as well. We will discuss about this situation with more focus in next part of the chapter. Before that we should know how our Chagrin is affected by COMPANY.

We often take out someone's anger on someone else.

Sometimes parents have to bear the consequences of fighting between friends. We shout at our parents in anger which can affect their emotions and we all know what happens if we affect their emotions....! In this way somewhere the Company becomes the cause of our Chagrin.

Now, it is necessary for us to talk on a matter that why we need COMPANY in our path to success. Look, it is not necessary that the company which is good for others should also be good for us. It may be possible that, that company may cause problems in achieving our goals by putting the wrong impact on us. So now the question arises that how will we know which company and friendship is good for us and which is not. People older than us often tell us to make friends with those who are better than you. But is it completely correct?

"There are only three things which increase
when shared: love, wisdom and happiness."
- Charbel Tadros

"Remember that your Heart-your Truth-will
never lead you astray. Let the Light of your
Heart guide your way."
- Valerie Rickel

"A company's goals are best achieved by helping workers or customers achieve their goals."
- Paul Jarvis

Why I have shown all these thoughts of some of the greatest writers to you? These quotes will let you know that this suggestion (make friends with those who are better than you.) of our elders is not completely correct. I am not telling you that there all suggestions are wrong but I don't know why I am little dissatisfied with this thing.

At this point, some of the people may get offended from me that how can you say this. Suggestions given by our elders is always correct, how can you decline it! And some people may say that the suggestion is completely correct for the present world. Everyone is obsessed with himself and all are selfish so, we should also be like that. But, for all these people, I have a simple and calm question, "How can you say that?"

You have not seen the whole world, right! I am completely agreed with you that the people whom we meet, most of them are selfish but "not all". Note this point "not all". Some of them are also kind and helpful. If you don't agree with this then I have some proves to show you.

Ok, tell me if all people are selfish then how there are more than 10 million NGOs in the whole world.

If you want to know about our country India then how there are more than 50,000 NGOs in India.

I am just telling you that from my perspective this suggestion is little incomplete. Let's see whether we can complete it or not! I know that in today's time no one belongs to anyone, everyone cares about their work, even all of us are also mean. But despite being selfish, we can help others. for example; If there is a child who is a little behind you in studies and there is no one to help him. If you help him in this situation, then reversely you will also benefit from it. But, how?

Suppose if you help that child in his studies then, somewhere you too will be revisited to the chapters and may be the topic which you may have forgotten, you will get a quick look at it. Many will say that, this is the wastage of time but if you observe it, you will find that it is really beneficial to you. But, you also have to take a precaution here. Be assured that the child will not disturb you while your studies. Our elders tell us to be friends with people who are better than us so that we can be benefitted but, "BOONAGE" tells us to make friendship with those children also who are not much better than us because they will help us more than the children who are better from us.

But, time to time we must check whether our company is helping us to grow and to reach our goal quickly or taking us away from our goal. No matter what happens, we always have to keep this thing in mind that nothing can take us away from our goal. And the answer to one of the main question that our COMPANY or FRIENDS' CIRCLE is good or bad is very simple and clear. We all should understand that anything is good till it is helpful for us and we are also helpful to that but, when that thing start affecting us and our goal becomes bad even curse for us.

And yeah, remember a thing that it is more important to know that which things can take us down rather to know which things can take us up because generally a single principle is responsible for a person's success but a lot more things are responsible for a person's failure.

CHAPTER SEVEN

Unreal World

Having learned about the company and its effects in our lives, we will turn to a very important aspect of teenage. All the lessons we have seen so far are the magic of our real life, but this lesson will make us aware of the maze of our Imagination World. All of us teenagers are living two lives at the same time. One is our physical world and one is our mental world. The lessons so far, even the coming lessons will teach you how to deal with the physical world, but what about our mental world? It is also very important for us to know about this because as much as the physical world affects our goal, our mental world does more. Likewise, I know that I am not the only child who, when the teacher is teaching the class, I am lost in a different psychic world and remain in the same world until there is no interruption. Sometimes all these things sound very funny but this has bad impact as well. Personally, I have a lot of problems with this thing.

Once, in my maths class, when the teacher was teaching on stage, I was thinking something in my mind and was lost in some other world. But suddenly my friend sitting next to me pushed me hard and my pen fell down from my hand. I was shocked and started looking here and there. Then he told me what are you doing brother, where are you lost, the teacher has been calling you since then and you are sitting completely silent. I said "what?". Then the teacher asked me "are you alright?" I said "Yes!" and again class get started. At that time I was laughing at myself because when the teacher was teaching in the class, the thing going on in my mind was that why do people masturbate? I was laughing very loudly at myself but I was controlling it so that this laugh would not come out.

This is not the first time. This had happened to me many times. Sometimes in my mind I talked about something else, sometimes in Science class in Maths class, sometimes in Sst class in English class. Sometimes in my mind I would say that I am roaming here, sometimes in my mind that I am eating this.

After listening to this story, this question must be arising in our mind that why the name of this chapter or lesson is "Unreal World"?

The unreal world refers to our mental world in which we are not living in our present time. For example: Suppose I am playing and at that time there is a discussion going on in my mind related to studies. So in this condition the playground where I am playing is referring to my physical world i.e. towards my real world but my mind is pointing towards my mental world which is unreal world for me at that time. Anything can happen in our unreal world, whether it is studies, whether it is games, whether it is porn, whether it is sleep or much more.

Yeah, I know many of you must be thinking that why he is discussing about porn, masturbation and these types of things. And this should also be in your mind because often no one talks about it but in today's time, due to the surroundings around us and the things happening in it, teenagers get to know about all these things. There are some teenagers who ignore these things and go ahead, then there are some who get away from their aim due to this. They do not like to study or do any other work. And there are many more problems. And somehow, this becomes the unreal world for most teenagers.

We teenagers find these things very interesting and if we say that our company or our group of friends is involved in all these things, then we get involved in it even if we do not want to. Once we get involved in it, it has a great impact on our life but it is not that if we have all these things in our mind, then we will be clearly separated from the rest of the world. We will not feel like doing anything. Our life will be in turmoil. We will completely deviate from our aim. There is nothing like that.

If we have a strong determination to change ourselves, then we can do anything. If we are more involved in all these things then we can apply "21 days rule" on ourselves. We will definitely talk about what this "21 days rule" is, but before that we should know what will happen with it. By applying "21 days rule" we will get away from any of our distractions if we follow it strictly. Even, we will get closer to our aim and our mind will also be removed from all these things but, something or the other will remain. Because once the thing that settles in our mind, we can make it stand but we cannot remove it. And why even remove it? Is this something wrong? Have we committed any crime knowing about it? Does it have nothing to do with our lives?

There is a simple answer to all these questions: "No!" If you are thinking that all these things are wrong, or knowing that you have committed any crime or you do not want to know further about these things, then you are wrong.

And as of now, the better control you have over your mind, the better you will be able to handle this thing. And the way to control your mind is "21 days rule". But what is this?

• 21 Days Rule:
Scientific research says that if you follow any particular thing or a particular routine continuously for 21 days, then you get used to that thing or that routine. I have also followed this thing and seriously it works very well. You all should follow this. If you follow your strict routine regularly for 21 days, then the first thing is that you will be more happy than before and the second thing is that you will also get away from your distraction.

Now the thing is, it is easy to say but very difficult to follow continuously. Well, this problem is for a teenager, not for a boonager.

DISTRACTION

Distraction is an alarm,
Which keeps you awake.

Distraction is the reason,
Why you reach your place.

Distraction is a way,
To check yourself.

Distraction is an evil,
With good effects as well.

If you take this literally,
Distraction is everything to keep yourself alive.

- Aditya Aman Jha

CHAPTER EIGHT

A sweet tragedy

So here arrives one of the most interesting lesson of "BOONAGE" which will be also a lot humorous when you think about it in your future or say, in college life. "A SWEET TRAGEDY" Many of you must be wondering about the name of this chapter.

So like the rest of the chapters, we will start this chapter again with a question. Why did we name this chapter "A SWEET TRAGEDY"?

What most teenagers find most sweet in their teenage years is love or in other words, love at first sight. Please don't take it like I am making fun of it. Seriously, I am not doing it. There is no problem in this, at all! If someone is telling you that" This is wrong. You should not do this. This is none of your business. Or anything else." Don't take it seriously until your inner soul tells you that "you are doing wrong." And make sure that the day when you get this voice from your inner soul, leave the thing immediately at the moment.

We can apply this principle on various other activities of our life as well. Especially, when we are studying; sometimes, we feel bored and don't want to study. You can apply this principle there also. Analyse yourself and your mistakes. And start studying again. But, this time don't repeat the mistakes you have done earlier.

Back to the topic again, we were experiencing that we should stop involving things in our life which are not supported by our inner soul. But, we do and that's why it's called "A SWEET TRAGEDY".

The main problem is not that we get feelings about the person in front or we are getting attracted towards someone. The main problem is that in the case of most teenagers, all these things are sham. Most teenagers want to be in a relationship to be cool in front of everyone and to show off. Somehow it puts a very hard impact on their studies and their goals, which most of us teenagers treat lightly.

Here the real problem arrives.From here we start doing the work that affects our aim. And we don't have to do the same thing.

This question must be coming in the mind of many of you that why do I always keep saying that listen to your inner soul, listen to your inner soul. Many of you must have heard a saying that "A woodcutter does not wield an ax on his own foot." If you understand the meaning of this saying, then you will also understand the meaning of my saying that "Listen to your inner soul".

Look, all I have to say is that we should do everything,reprobation , fun, play-jumping everything but up to a limit. We should keep the validity of every work in our daily life till our aim. All that we are doing at the end will give us a final output which will either be very good or very bad according to our doings. Either there will be regrets in our life or there will be joyful memories. Everything is in our hands.

Rewind the poetry of our first chapter "Who Am I ?". You will get to know what I am saying. In starting we feel that all these things are not affecting us and our aim, but in actual, all these things affect our aim a lot.

If we take all these things too seriously but at the same time, it is just a source of entertainment for the person in front, then this thing hurts us a lot. And this is right too. You can't do anything after the output comes.

• REMEMBER ONE THING:
INPUT IS IN OUR HAND
BUT OUTPUT IS IN THE HANDS OF
INPUT.

So the more input you give towards your aim, the more better your output will be.

At the end, all I will say is that in life there is nothing sweeter than sugar and things made from it. So, eat sugar with no tragedy.

"They do not love that do not show their love. The course of true love never did run smooth. Love is a familiar. Love is a devil. There is no evil angel but love."
- William Shakespeare

CHAPTER NINE

Depression and Dedication

Let's start our chapter with a similar question which is asked throughout the whole book and that is why "DEPRESSION AND DEDICATION" is chosen as a step (8th step) towards turning our lovely teen into boon?

After all the adventures in our life, the result is usually only two things, either happiness with further motivation or sadness with lots of depression to cause mental pressure. Everyone talks about how to get happiness and how to live happily but no one discuss about the fact that how to stand against failure with calmness and peace. So here we are to discuss this thing as well..!

According to a survey, it's estimated that one in every five adolescents from all walks of life will suffer from depression at some point during their teen years. Here are some results in front of you, let's have a look at it:

•Despite what many believe, mental illness is common in teenagers.

•Approximately one in five teens (aged 12 to 18) suffer from at least one mental health disorder.

•Every 100 minutes a teen takes their own life.

•Suicide is the third-leading cause of death for young people ages 15 to 24.

•About 20 percent of all teens experience depression before they reach adulthood.

•Between 10 to 15 percent suffer from symptoms at any one time.

•Only 30 percent of depressed teens are being treated for it.

I am not scaring you, I am just making you aware about the recent situation of teenagers in our world. This is a very serious problem and we need to focus on it because every life is as important as oxygen and trees. We can't let them die.

Not only one thing is actually responsible for your depression and inner dissatisfaction. Somewhere, a lot of things happening around you can cause you to think about it and suddenly you get involved in it.

And you all should note a point that INVOLVEMENT INCREASE DEPRESSION(mathematical involvement is directly proportional to depression).

The more things you involve in, the more you will be distracted, the more your problems will get increased and the final outcome will be depression.

So the first step which we all should take is,"Reduce your involvement from a lot of things which is useless to you and most importantly your goal." You will feel like you are living more happy than before and are more focused towards your work. Even, you will feel much better than earlier.

Secondly the main thing which you all must follow is introduce new things in your life. Like: singing, dancing, etc. If you have to pass your time you can also learn new languages like: French, Spanish etc. It seems to be interesting and helpful for us. Why I am telling you to do this?
It will automatically help you to decrease involvement and useless interactions with people. And you will also get a new thing to show off in front of your colleagues that you have learnt a new talent which is not in them. I bet this show off is much better than the show off of your boyfriend or girlfriend and ultimately it will help you to.

Some talents like: singing and dancing can even help you in the situations when you are feeling sad. Humming the song can increase the secretion of dopamine(hormone which make you feel happy) and you will feel relaxed. If you love tech then you can also learn coding, this will surely help you a lot.

All these things are such steps which will help us to get into depression but what should we do when we are already stressed or depressed. Personally, I feel more relaxed in these situations while listening the songs which I love. You can do the things which make you feel happy and you also live to do that. Some people love to draw, some love to listen songs, some love to dance and some love to cook. It's our personal choice. But, this is not enough. If these things can't help you then you can do something different which is all time favourite for everyone, I guess.

Just take a nap of 1-2 hours and you will feel good. But, it's little hard.In this condition we do not sleep quickly. If this isn't working then you can also go for a walk but the place must be peaceful. All these things will help you a lot.

Read this passage from the book "BEYOND BLUE" written by Therese J. Borchard.

"In my opinion, it's all of the above and more," writes Therese J. Borchard, author of Beyond Blue. "Most experts would agree with me that there is more stress today than in previous generations. Stress triggers depression and mood disorders, so that those who are predisposed to it by their creative wiring or genes are pretty much guaranteed some symptoms of depression at the confusing and difficult time of adolescence. I think modern lifestyles -lack of community and family support, less exercise, no casual and unstructured technology-free play, less sunshine and more computer -factors into the equation."

Borchard also wonders about the role of environmental factors such as diets of American processed fast foods and the possibility of increased exposure to toxins. She speculates that even if our brains are similar to research subjects in the past, our hectic lifestyles, environmental toxins, and other challenges may increase the stress factors that contribute to depression.

Some more fabulous poetries and words for you which will make you feel motivated:
• A LESSON
There's a girl who smiles all the time, to show the world that she is fine.

A boy who surrounds himself with friends, wishes that his life would end.

For those who say they never knew, the saddest leave the least of clues.
- LANG LEAV
Believe me, every heart has its secret sorrows. which the world knows not. And oftentimes we call a man cold, when he is only sad.
-HENRY WADSWORTH LONGFELLOW

All these passages and poetries from some of the famous writers is provided in this book "BOONAGE" to let you know the secrets of yourself and your powers from which you are unaware.

The main point is we should always be ready to face the challenges in our life. Our life is full of challenges and we can't move away from them. They are in every part of our life. If we skip them right now they will create problems for us in future but will come in our life for sure.

Mostly, we all get depressed mainly in two situations:
• Failure
• We don't get the thing which we want.

Remember a thing that a successful person is not just made up of lot of victory in his life. They have faced a lot of failures in their life which they use as steps for success in their life. This is called "DEDICATION". It will never let to down. Always trust on your self and remember one more thing that "SUCCESS NEED SACRIFICES". You have to give it and show your power that who you are and what you can do for your goal.

Let the world know you for your DEDICATION AND FAILURES which have make you a successful person today.
 • CHALLENGES ARE THE PATH TO SUCCEESS IN OUR LIFE

CHAPTER TEN

Personality and Impressions

Finally, we are very close to end of the book or you can say end of the steps for transforming our whore teen into boon. One last time, let's take a look at a similar question, "WHY?"

Why we have selected "PERSONALITY AND IMPRESSION" as a step towards turning our teen into boon and more necessarily why this is selected as a last chapter in our whole journey?

We have selected "PERSONALITY AND IMPRESSION" as a step towards turning our teen into boon because it not only makes a person seem better but also enhances their overall personality. It is necessary for every field of life. Good impressions do not vanish easily rather stay for a very long time. They say that a person has something unique and is confident enough. If we know how to create impression from very beginning of our age then it will help us a lot in our future like: in business, in job etc. Everywhere, Impression plays an important role. It makes us feel confident and provokes our personality. That's why we have selected "PERSONALITY AND IMPRESSION" as one of our steps towards turning our teen into boon.

Now, why we have selected this as a last chapter? The reason for this is simple, what we already have, we should use it well first, after that new things should be learned. All the lessons we have seen so far were already inside us and were affecting us badly but Impression is such a thing which will be applied in our day-to-day life after learning it through various sources.

Personality can be the most powerful strength and weapon of a person which can boost one's inner confidence and also make you feel more happy and motivated.

Hope so, you all have got the answer of "WHY?". Now we have to know the answer of "HOW?".

How can we improve our Personality and Impression in perspective of modern society? Let us know about it.

• First of all you all have to take the tough decision in yourself that I have to change myself and improve my personality and outlook. I am saying this because after this no one else will put pressure on you, but you yourself will focus on your outlook, diet and conversation skills. You will start searching the ways to improve your skills from various sources. You will become attentive towards yourself and point out your own mistakes.

"Never let yourself be a product of your surroundings, but encourage your surroundings to be a product of your personality"

• Secondly, we all have to become a good listener who can listen one's speech with patience. It will not only help us to improve our personality, it will also save you from bad situations. You should develop the habit of listening carefully to others rather than answering them, by this you can find solutions in even the worst situations. If someone is telling you something, then listen carefully to his words and then reply. This thing has a deep impact on your personality. Even if the person in front of you is very angry then he will calm down after seeing your behavior. This is a great way by which you can impress anyone.

"LET YOUR THOUGHTS EXPLAIN YOUR SUCCESS PATH"

• Third, You have to become patient. Reading new books will help you a lot and your knowledge will also increase. There are many benefits of reading books. This improves your focus and concentration power. It will improve your conversation skills and you will also get introduced to various now words. We all should take special care that while talking to anyone, we neither speak too fast nor too slowly. We have to learn to select good and good words and take special care of talking. Here we have come one step closer to creating our impression.

"READING" IS IMPORTANT.
IF YOU
KNOW HOW TO READ,
THEN THE WHOLE
WORLD OPENS UP
" TO YOU."
- BARACK OBAMA

• Fourth, If you want to develop your personality then one of the biggest step that all of you have to take is that you have to stop comparing yourself to others. Just understand a point that you are unique and you have some different talent in yourself. If you stop comparing yourself to others then it has many benefits. It has more chances that you can perform better than others. If you want to compare, then you should compare yourself with your own past. It will help you to know that in which field you have improved and in which field you have become worse. This is much better. Somewhere, comparison is also a reason behind stress and depression. So, you can also get out of it.

"Personality begins where comparison leaves off.

- Shannon L. Alder

• Fifth, Explore new things and meet new people. It will boost your confidence and you will also know various things about the cultural heritage of different groups of our society. The biggest thing you will get happiness and you will be able to do your work better.

Enough. If we follow all these steps properly, then we don't need to follow various rules and regulations and we will learn something for which many people attend the course and that is:

"PERSONALITY DEVELOPMENT"

Epilogue For Mature You

So finally, after listening to so many kitsch, all our lessons are on the stage of completion and now the time has come that we should conclude our complete book in some main points which must be life changing for us. So, do it.

1. Always trust yourself rather than the other person.

2. If you can dream, you can achieve.

3. Always listen to your soul, it will never discourage you.

4. The Best Never Competes. Don't try to compare yourself with anyone else.

5. Always feel yourself unique, you are the one who can change everything.

6. Just feel the power of a teenager, power of a growing tree.

7. Others can influence you, but they can't inspire you.

8. There is a huge difference between copying and following.

9. Present of a successful person is not successful rather his restless past, hardworking past and consistent focused past is successful.

10. We should obey the principles of somebody (ideal) in life but, simply getting influenced is not beneficial.

11. Anything is good for us and our future to a limited extent, but as the effect of that thing increases, we and our future come in danger. Everyone get affected through it.

12. You get birth and start living, But it requires lot more HARDWORK to build an empire with your PERSONALITY!

13. If you want that you should not be addicted to anything, then the most important emotional thing that should be inside you is "control over yourself".

14. If you listen to your inner soul, it will neither allow you to become addicted to any activity nor will it ever allow you to become addicted to any person.

15. Trust me,a lumberjack never attack on his own foot with axe for fun!

16. Be calm otherwise one will make you fool any day.

17. 3I's of "COMPANY"
•IMPORTANCE
• IMPACT
• INVOLVEMENT

18. Not only in our teenage, but "COMPANY" is the most important necessity in our whole life.

19. Chagrin and Addiction is affected by COMPANY.

20. It is not necessary that the company which is good for

others should also be good for us.

21. There are only three things which increase
when shared: love, wisdom and happiness."
- Charbel Tadros

22. Remember that your Heart-your Truth-will
never lead you astray. Let the Light of your
Heart guide your way.
- Valerie Rickel

23. A company's goals are best achieved by helping workers
or customers achieve their goals.
- Paul Jarvis

24. "BOONAGE" tells us to make friendship with those
children also who are not much better than us because they
will help us more than the children who are better from us.

25. Time to time we must check whether our company is
helping us to grow and to reach our goal quickly or taking
us away from our goal.

26. Remember a thing that it is more important to know
that which things can take us down rather to know which
things can take us up because generally a single principle is
responsible for a person's success but a lot more things are
responsible for a person's failure.

27. Always choose the thing which satisfies you and make
your soul happy.

28. Your first love or

Your future, Your goal, Your life.
Nothing is right or wrong. There correctness depends upon their use.

29. Enjoy your individual beauty and uniqueness; never wish that it would change.
- Geneveive C. Coulson

30. Anger can rage 'til it tears you apart, but the power of your smile can mend a broken heart.
- Malia Taitte

31. Love can leave you empty, love can make you whole. Love can make or break you. Love is in your soul.
- John Peter Read

32. Wisdom comes, but it takes time and experience. It takes care and love and utter obedience.
- Refinnej

33. Remember a thing that a successful person is not just made up of lot of victory in his life. They have faced a lot of failures in their life which they use as steps for success in their life.

34. Success need sacrifices.

35. Challenges are the path to succeess in our life.

36. Involvement increase depression(mathematical involvement is directly proportional to depression).

37. Mostly, we all get depressed mainly in two situations:

• Failure
• We don't get the thing which we want.

38. Let your thoughts explain your success path.

39. Personality can be the most powerful strength and weapon of a person which can boost one's inner confidence and also make you feel more happy and motivated.

40. Never let yourself be a product of your surroundings, but encourage your surroundings to be a product of your personality!

41. Personality begins where comparison leaves off.

- Be unique.
- Be memorable.
- Be confident.
- Be proud.

42. Last but not the least, main motive of our book "BOONAGE" is not to earn money. We just want to create awareness among teenagers who are frustrated from their life.

THANKS A MILLION TO ALL MY DEAR READERS